THE BEST BOOK OF

Nighttime Animals

Belinda Weber

KINGFISHER

BOSTON

Contents

KINGFISHER

a Houghton Mifflin Company imprint
222 Berkeley Street
Boston, Massachusetts 02116
www.houghtonmifflinbooks.com

Consultant: David Burnie
Managing editor: Carron Brown
Coordinating editor: Caitlin Doyle
Art director: Mike Davis
Assistant designer: Jack Clucas
DTP coordinator: Catherine Hibbert
DTP operator: Claire Cessford
Production controller: Jessamy Oldfield

Illustrations by Mark Bergin

First published in 2006

10 9 8 7 6 5 4 3 2 1

1TR/0206/WKT/SCHOY/128KMA/C

LIBRARY OF CONGRESS CATALOGING-IN-
PUBLICATION DATA
Weber, Belinda.
The best book of nighttime animals/by
Belinda Weber.—1st ed.
    p. cm.
1. Nocturnal animals—Juvenile literature.
I. Title.
QL755.5W43   2006
591.5'18—dc22

                    2005027201

ISBN 0-7534-5985-X
ISBN 978-07534-5985-0

Printed in China

Why are some animals active at night?

In the darkness of night most animals head for the safety of their homes or find a quiet place to sleep. But others, called nocturnal animals, wake up and become active. They may need the cooler temperature that night brings in order to survive. Or they may prefer to lurk in the shadows, safely away from predators.

Hunter and hunted

Cats are hunters that eat mice. They listen out for tiny sounds that tell them where to find their prey. Mice also have good hearing. They listen for the sounds of hunters.

Seeking heat

Pit vipers do not need to see their prey. They have special holes called pits on their lips that detect heat. The snake can track an animal by its body heat.

Pit

Life in the dark

Nocturnal animals often have larger eyes and ears to help them find their way in the dark. Frogs and toads need to stay cool to stop their skin from drying out. They stay out of the sunshine during the day and become more active at night.

Tree frogs can dry out in the fierce sun, so they are active at night.

Fennec foxes have large ears and can hear very well.

Tarsiers have big eyes that help them see well in the dark.

5

The jungle at night

In the jungles of South America many animals wake up when night falls. When howler monkeys call out to each other, their voices can be heard from up to three miles away. They are especially noisy at sunrise and sunset, when their loud, roaring sounds let each other know where they are.

The owl monkey, or douroucouli, leaps from tree to tree, looking for insects and fruits to eat.

Howler monkeys

Three-toed
sloth

Active in shifts

By coming out at night, nocturnal animals
avoid all the creatures that are active during the
day. This means that they will not eat each
other or compete for the same food. By
avoiding each other, all the animals
can eat from the same trees.

Olingo

Owl monkey

Silky anteater

Desert life

The North American desert is extremely hot during the day, so most animals come out at night. They spend their days in cool burrows or dens or asleep in shady places. The skin that covers their ears is thin, so the blood vessels are close to the surface. This helps the creatures stay cool.

Stink bombs

Skunks have an unusual way of defending themselves against attacks. They squirt a jet of smelly liquid from underneath their tails. This makes it hard for the attacker to breathe, and the skunk can escape.

Little owl

Deer

Skunk

Scorpion

Cricket

8

Nighthawk

Little owl

Coyotes

Kangaroo rat

Kit fox

9

Wild dogs

Wolves, jackals, and dingos are all wild dogs. They have excellent vision and a good sense of smell. These senses help them track down their prey and also stay together in a pack. Wolves are well known for their eerie howling at the moon. This tells the others in the group where they are and helps them stay in touch. They also use their tails and faces to communicate with each other and hunt together as a pack.

Jackals

Wolves

Hyenas

Sharing food

Jackals and hyenas are scavengers as well as hunters. They hunt for themselves and will also follow lions to steal their prey or finish their leftovers. Hyenas have a doglike shape, but they are not wild dogs.

Howling dogs

Dingos howl like wolves to communicate with each other. They hunt small mammals on their own, but they will join other dingos to hunt larger prey.

Strong hunters

Wolves are built to hunt. Their long, strong legs help them run great distances. Wolves have big stomachs, so they can eat a lot at one time. They gorge themselves after a successful hunt, eating as much as 20 pounds of meat in one meal.

Dingo

Woodlands at night

When night falls in the woodlands of northern Europe, not everything goes to sleep. Hedgehogs begin looking for food. Foxes are clever hunters. They listen for prey and then sneak up on it. They can move their ears in the direction of a sound and can even hear small animals digging under the ground.

Eating worms

Badgers spend their days asleep in a burrow called a set, or sett. They rummage through the leaf litter at night looking for earthworms, insects, and snails to eat.

Twilight zone

Deer settle down in clearings for the night. They are shy creatures and are at their most active during late evenings and early mornings.

Male fallow deer grow antlers, which are made of bone.

Hedgehog

Mole

Woodlice

Hiding during the day

Moths fly around at night, in order to avoid birds that might eat them. Their mottled colors help them blend in with bark or leaves while they rest during the day.

Moths

Tawny owl

Every evening badgers leave their sets to look for food.

Red fox

Night birds

Owls are hunters that catch their prey at night. They listen out for the tiny squeaks and rustling sounds that small mammals make as they search for food in the undergrowth. Once they have found their prey, owls swoop through the air to catch it. They have sharp claws on their feet called talons, which they use to grab their victims, and sharp beaks to tear up the flesh.

Barn owl

Long-eared owl

Silent hunters

Many owls have soft, fluffy fringes on their wing feathers. These help the owls fly silently and pounce on their victims without being heard. In the quiet of the night the owl can concentrate on listening for sounds of its animal prey.

Big ears

Long-eared owls prefer to hunt in the open countryside. Like most owls, one of their ear holes is slightly higher up than the other. This helps them figure out exactly where a sound is coming from so that they can home in on their prey. Long-eared owls spend their days resting in trees.

Slow flier

Barn owls have flat, heart-shaped faces with
big eyes. Their hearing is excellent, and they
use their ears to find their rodent prey.
Once they have found a victim, they
fly slowly, quietly, and close
to the ground until
they catch it.

15

Moonlit seas

Even in the murky depths of the seas day and night are important. Some fish spend their days in the calm, deep waters but then rise up to the surface to eat when it is quiet at night. Others swim close to the surface during the day and return to deeper water overnight. Whether swimming up or down, the fish must always swim past other fish that want to eat them.

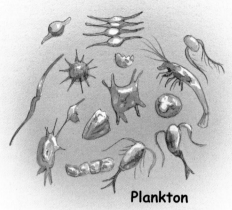

Plankton

Herring

Dangerous jelly

Common jellyfish follow small fish on their nightly journeys up to the surface. Any fish that brushes against a jellyfish's stinging tentacles is paralyzed and eaten.

Tiny plankton

Millions of tiny animals called plankton rise up through the water to eat at the surface each evening. Thousands of other fish follow the plankton to the top to feast on them and each other.

Toothy hunters

Whitetip reef sharks cruise through the moonlit water looking for food. They sleep during the day, hiding in caves or lurking on the seabed, to avoid any predators that might eat them.

Wetlands

Rivers, swamps, and wetlands provide homes for many nocturnal animals. Otters, alligators, frogs, and toads hunt at night, making use of the darkness to help them find their prey. The flowing water of a river offers a variety of places for animals to find food or shelter. However, animals have to be careful that they are not washed away.

Snappy hunter

American alligators are huge, growing up to 18 feet long. They are not fussy eaters and will feed on anything they can catch, including turtles and birds.

Staying dry

Otters eat fish and spend a lot of their time in the river chasing after them. Their fur is waterproof, and their feet are webbed to help them swim. They are excellent swimmers, and they use their flattened tails like rudders to help them steer.

Saving some for later

Water voles make their nests next to the river. They are good swimmers and eat water plants, roots, bulbs, and fallen fruits. They occasionally store extra food in their nests.

American alligator

Noisy neighbors

When a bullfrog searches for a mate, the male "calls" loudly. It has a pouch underneath its chin that blows up like a balloon. This makes the sound much louder so that it can be heard from farther away.

19

Furry fliers

Bats are shy creatures that fly at night to avoid birds that might eat them otherwise. During the day these animals stay hidden away, roosting in caves, trees, or under the roofs of buildings. Bats are the only mammals that can fly. Their wings are made of skin that is stretched between the bats' long fingers. Different types of bats eat different foods. Many feed on fruits and flowers, but others are hunters.

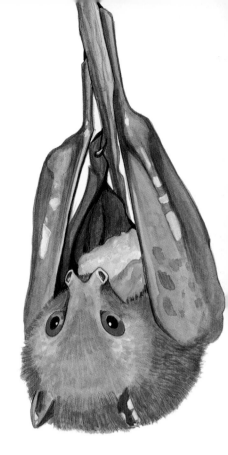

Messy eaters

Fruit bats squash fruits into their mouths, drinking the juice. They drop any seeds or pulp onto the ground.

Listening for food

Some bats let out a high-pitched squeak. If this sound hits an insect, some of the sound bounces back. The echo lets the bat know where its food is. This is called echolocation.

An echo of a bat's squeak lets it know where its insect prey is.

Sounds like lunch

Long-eared bats hunt insects that fly at night. They can move their large ears in many directions to pick up even the quietest sounds.

Blood for dinner

Vampire bats are shy and nervous. They land close to a cow and then scurry closer, crawling on their wings. They bite their victims with sharp teeth, then lap up the blood. Vampire bats prefer cows' blood, but they will occasionally bite humans.

An African night

Darkness brings many predators out onto the African plains. Baboons settle down to sleep in nests that are made high up in the trees. Hippopotamuses leave the cool water of lakes, where they wallow during the day to stop their skin from burning in the sun's heat. When it is cooler at night, they come out to graze on the lush grasses.

Safety in numbers
With leopards and lions hunting them, gazelles gather in large herds. This means that many eyes and ears are able to listen out for danger

Gazelles

Hippopotamuses

Baboons

Mongooses have thick
fur to protect them
from snakes, which
they hunt for food.

Leopard

Royal python

Mongooses

23

Cat empire

Many big cats sneak up on their prey while they are asleep at night. Like other big cats, tigers have soft, fleshy pads on their feet that help them walk quietly, letting them creep up on their prey. Many cats' eyes have long, thin pupils that look like slits. In the dark these slits widen to let in as much light as possible. This helps the cats see in the moonlight so that they can hunt their prey.

Hunted
Ocelots' beautifully patterned fur attracts high prices in the fashion world. So many of these cats have been killed that this trade has now been banned.

Water cats

South American jaguars like to eat fish, which they scoop out of the water with their large paws. Unlike many cats, jaguars love water and are very good swimmers.

Night in the bush

In the heat of the Australian bush many animals prefer the cooler temperatures at night. Echidnas snuffle around, searching for ants and termites, which they suck up with their long tongues. They are good diggers and can break open termites' nests with their strong claws. Kangaroos travel to new feeding grounds at night, covering longer distances than they could during the day.

Giant heads

Cassowaries are large birds that live in Australia's rain forests and are active at sunrise and sunset. They have large, bony shields called casques on the tops of their heads. These protect their heads as they push their way through plants.

Kangaroos

Opossum

Sugar
glider

Koala

Phalanger

Sleepy koala
Koalas eat eucalyptus leaves,
which are hard to digest.
The koala does not get much
energy from its food so it
sleeps a lot. It does not need
to drink very often, since it
gets all the moisture it needs
from its leafy food. Koala
is an aboriginal word
that means "no drink."

Echidna

27

Bugs galore

Thousands of bugs wake up at night to search for food. They creep, scurry, and slither around, trying not to be seen by anything that might eat them. The only time they make themselves seen or heard is when they are looking for a mate. Crickets sing noisily to tell others where they are. Glowworms flash pulses of light, signaling their position to others.

Hairy legs

Goliath tarantulas, or giant bird-eating spiders, hunt at night. Hairs on their legs pick up vibrations in the air, alerting them to their prey moving closeby.

Stinging tails

Scorpions are sneaky hunters that lurk close to their lairs, waiting for prey to creep by. They grab their victim with their pincerlike claws or paralyze them with their poisonous stinging tails.

Creepy cockroach

Cockroaches are one of the fastest insects. When they are threatened, they dart into dark cracks to hide.

Poisonous claws

Centipedes have sharp, poisonous claws that act like fangs. The poison is strong enough to kill small mammals.

Female glowworms have an organ underneath their abdomens that makes light to attract males.

Slimy slitherers

Slugs and snails can dry up in the heat of the sun, so they find food at night. They slither across the ground on a layer of slippery wet mucus.

Night flights

Moths fly at night, stopping at flowers to suck up nectar through their coiled tongues.

Crickets sing by rubbing their wings together.

Raiders of the night

Animals need space to live, but people need to build houses to make homes for themselves.

Many animals have learned to live among people. Gardens and parks have become their homes, and animals feed on the scraps of food that are left behind, as well as the plants that grow there. Rats and mice find plenty to eat out of people's leftovers, and larger animals, such as foxes and raccoons, raid garbage cans.

Hungry raccoons

Raccoons are woodland creatures, but they have learned to live with humans. They have a good sense of smell and are excellent climbers. They can get into garbage cans and often feast on leftover food.

Raccoon

Rats

Glossary

abdomen The third, or rear, part of an insect's body.

aboriginal Aborigines were the first people to live in Australia. Aboriginal describes something that has come from the aborigines.

bush Open scrublands in Australia.

communicate To pass messages between one another with sounds or body language.

competing Trying to outdo another to find food or a mate.

detect To find.

digest To absorb nutrients and energy from food.

mammal A warm-blooded animal that feeds milk to its young.

mottled Irregular patterns or markings on the skin that help break up an animal's shape.

mucus Slime that is produced by the body.

paralyzed Unable to move.

predator An animal that hunts and kills other animals for food.

prey Animals that are hunted and eaten by other animals.

pupils The black parts of eyes that open to let in light.

rodent A small mammal such as a mouse or a rat.

rudder A device that is used to help steer a boat.

scavenger An animal that eats food that is already dead.

tentacles Long, frilly strings or legs.

track To find and follow.

trade The buying and selling of goods, in this case, animal skins.

undergrowth Small plants and leaf litter that are found close to the ground.

vibrations Movements in the air that help a predator find its prey.

31

Index